Rocks and soils

A brief history

TODAY... 1830 In Britain, Charles Lyell states that the Earth is hundreds of millions of years old (it is now known to be 4.6 billion years old)... 1822 Friedrich Mohs of Germany makes up a scale for the hardness of materials. It goes from 1 to 10... 1797 Sir James Hall, in Britain, proves that volcanic lava cools to make rock... 1785 In Britain, James Hutton shows that the rocks of the past were formed in the same way as rocks are forming today. As a result, he believes the Earth is extremely old. Hutton becomes known as the father of geology... 1779 Horace de Saussure, in France, invents the word geology for the study of the Earth's rocks... 1776 James Keir, in Britain, suggests that many rocks are produced from volcanoes... 1774 Abraham Werner, in Germany, works out a way to compare and sort out the minerals that make up the world's rocks. He uses properties such as colour and hardness. He states that rocks are made of layers, with the oldest at the bottom and the youngest at the top. Before this everyone thought that all rocks were the same age. He also says that some rocks were formed from sand and mud settling out of the sea bed... 1650 Archbishop Usher, in Britain, uses the Bible to work out that the Earth and its rocks were all formed in 4004BC...

For more information visit www.curriculumvisions.com

Word list

These are some science words that you should look out for as you go through the book. They are shown using CAPITAL letters.

ABSORB
To soak up.

ACID
A liquid that destroys many materials, including rocks. Vinegar is a very weak acid. Rain water is an extremely weak acid.

BRICK
A block of clay that has been baked in an oven (a kiln).

CEMENT
A powder, made partly from baked limestone, that is added to water to make a kind of glue for holding rocks together.

CHALK
A soft, white and very pure kind of limestone rock. It absorbs water easily.

CLAY
A soft, sticky material made of pieces of rock too fine to see without a microscope.

CONCRETE
A mixture of cement, sand and stones.

GRANITE
A hard, white or grey-coloured rock speckled with black.

LAVA
The name for both the liquid that is erupted from a volcano and the cooled rock. Lava rock has tiny bubbles in it.

LIMESTONE
A hard, grey or cream-coloured rock made of the remains of the shells of ancient sea creatures.

LOAM
A soil which is an even mixture of all sizes of particles from sand to clay.

MARBLE
A type of limestone rock baked underground. It is often white with coloured veins running through it.

MUD
The name for fine material in water.

PEBBLES
Rounded stones.

QUARRY
A place where building stone is dug up.

ROCK
A hard material made up of small pieces that have been melted or squashed together while deep underground.

SAND
Small pieces of rock, like the material found on a beach.

SANDSTONE
A rock made from cemented sand grains.

SLATE
A rock made of clay that breaks up into thin sheets.

SOIL
A mixture of stones, sand, clay and rotting plant and animal material.

STONE
A small piece of rock or a type of rock that is useful for building.

SUBSOIL
The layer of soil that lies between the surface layer and the rock below.

TOPSOIL
The top layer of a soil. It is darker than the layer below.

Weblink: www.curriculumvisions.com

Contents

	Page
Word list	**2**
Unit 1: Rock and soil	**4**
Unit 2: Rocks from volcanoes	**6**
Unit 3: Hard and soft rocks	**8**
Unit 4: Rocks shape the land	**10**
Unit 5: Rocks that soak up water	**12**
Unit 6: How rocks are used	**14**
Unit 7: Artificial rocks	**16**
Unit 8: Pebbles, sand and clay	**18**
Unit 9: Soils from rocks	**20**
Unit 10: Soils and water	**22**
Index	**24**

Weblink: www.curriculumvisions.com

Rock and soil

The Earth's surface is made of rocks, but they are mostly covered up with soils. You can find bare rocks if you know where to look.

Most of us rarely see large amounts of **ROCK**. This is very strange because the whole of the Earth's surface is made of rock. However, in most places the rocks are covered up by soil (Picture 1), so you have to know where to look to find them.

Rocks can be seen in seaside cliffs and in quarries (Picture 2). When you look into a **QUARRY** you can see that we live on a world of solid rock.

Rock and soil

Between us and rock there is a layer of soft, loose material. It is called **SOIL**. A soil is made of tiny pieces. Soil covers the rock. It is only a metre or so thick.

▼ (Picture 1) Soil is a thin layer on top of rock.

A handful of soil. It is a loose material.

Soil

A piece of rock. It is a solid material.

Rock

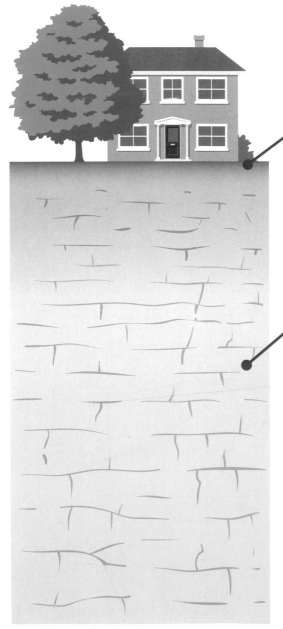

Weblink: www.curriculumvisions.com

▼ (Picture 2) This is a quarry in Cornwall. So much rock has been taken away that there is now a very deep hole.

At the top of the picture you will see houses. They help you to see how deep the quarry is.

Summary
- Rock is solid material, such as seen in a quarry.
- Soil lies on top of rock.

Q Which is on top of which: rock, soil?

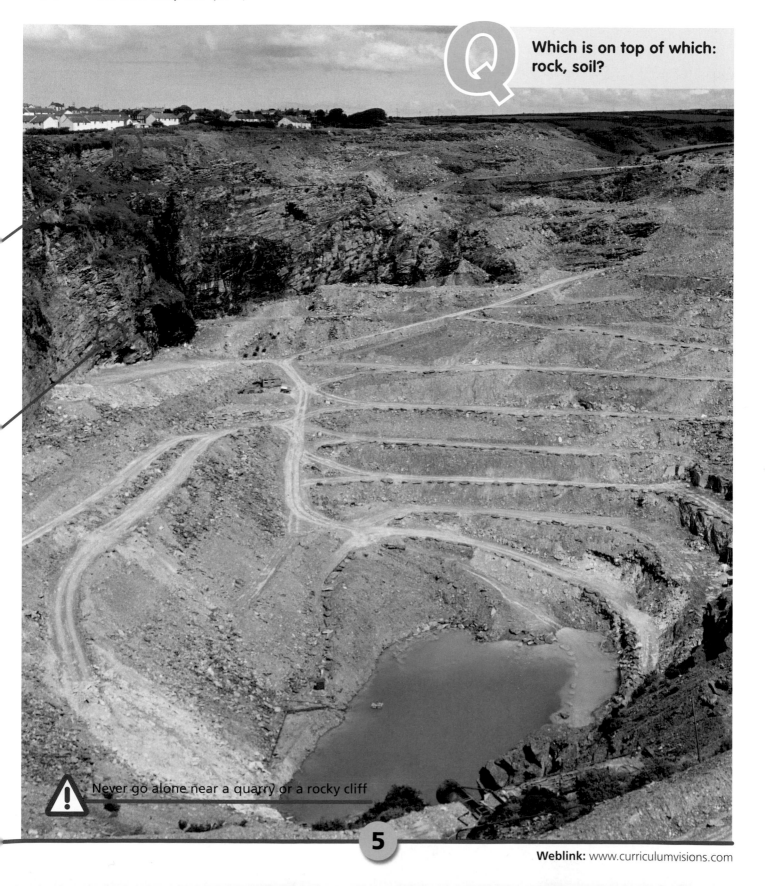

⚠ Never go alone near a quarry or a rocky cliff

Weblink: www.curriculumvisions.com

Rocks from volcanoes

Many rocks begin in the fiery fountains of volcanoes.

How do rocks come to make up the surface of the Earth? Many of them come from erupting volcanoes.

Liquid rock

Deep underground the rock is liquid. From time-to-time it bursts to the surface and forms a volcanic eruption (Pictures 1 and 2).

Lava

The runny material bursting from a volcano is called **LAVA**. It is red hot and flows over the land like a river (Picture 2). As it cools, however, it loses its red colour and turns black. The cooled material is hard rock (Picture 3).

▼ **(Picture 1) This is a volcano erupting lava.**

Weblink: www.curriculumvisions.com

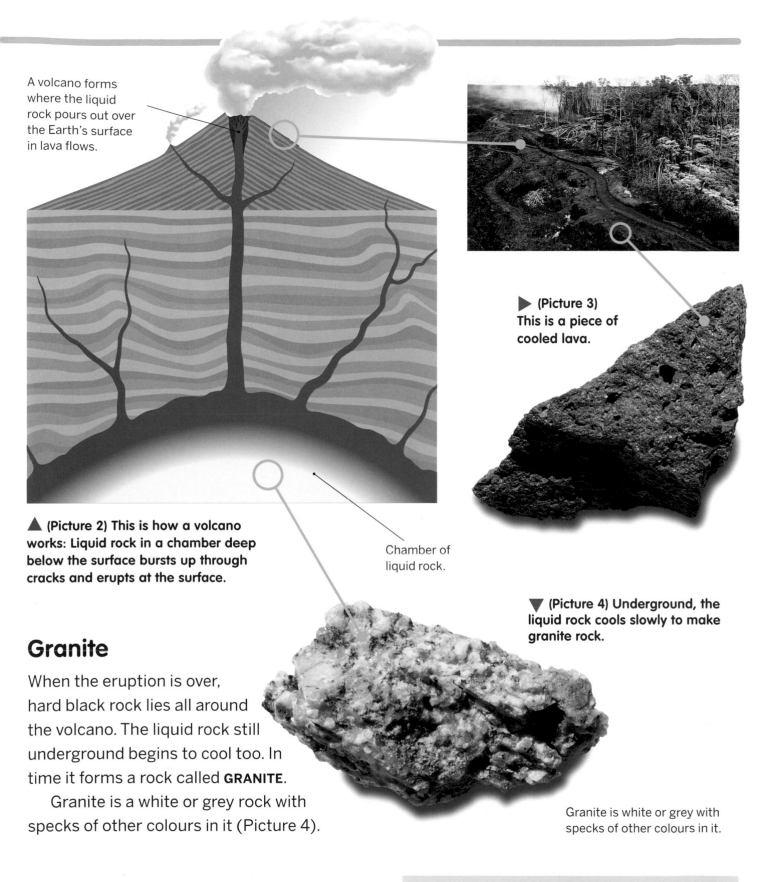

A volcano forms where the liquid rock pours out over the Earth's surface in lava flows.

▶ **(Picture 3) This is a piece of cooled lava.**

▲ **(Picture 2) This is how a volcano works: Liquid rock in a chamber deep below the surface bursts up through cracks and erupts at the surface.**

Chamber of liquid rock.

▼ **(Picture 4) Underground, the liquid rock cools slowly to make granite rock.**

Granite

When the eruption is over, hard black rock lies all around the volcano. The liquid rock still underground begins to cool too. In time it forms a rock called **GRANITE**.

Granite is a white or grey rock with specks of other colours in it (Picture 4).

Granite is white or grey with specks of other colours in it.

Where does the lava in a volcano come from?

Summary
- Volcanic rocks include lava and granite. All volcanic rocks are made from liquid rock.
- Granite is a hard, grey speckled rock.

Weblink: www.curriculumvisions.com

Hard and soft rocks

Some rocks are much harder than others. This affects how they are used.

There are many different kinds of rock. Some rocks come from volcanoes. Other rocks are made in different ways. They all vary in hardness. Only the really hard ones are useful in building.

Hard or soft?

A rock is made of small grains. The hardness of a rock depends on what these grains are made of and what kind of natural glue holds them together.

Rocks made of **MUD** (**CLAY** and water) have no 'glue' holding them together. They are nearly all soft (Picture 1).

Rocks made from **SAND** (Picture 2) or shells (Picture 3) are glued together by natural

▲ (Picture 2) A rock made from sand feels like the sand you find on a beach – and it is often the same colour, too. You can see the sand grains easily. The grains feel rough to the touch. This type of rock is called SANDSTONE.

◄ (Picture 1) Mud squashes into a soft rock we call mudstone or shale. Mud is so fine we can't see the grains. This kind of rock feels smooth to the touch.

cements. If the CEMENT is hard, the rock is hard, but if the cement is soft, the rock is soft.

Rocks that have been baked when deep underground are always very hard (Picture 4). MARBLE is one of these rocks.

Testing for rock hardness

It is not easy to tell which rocks are hard and which are soft just by looking at them. To find out whether one rock is harder than another we can rub rocks gently together and see which one rubs away (Picture 5). The one that rubs away is the softer rock.

Is mud a hard or a soft rock?

▲ (Picture 3) LIMESTONE is made from sea shells. It can be white or grey in colour. CHALK is a soft, very white form of limestone.

▼ (Picture 4) Marble has been baked into a very hard rock while deep underground.

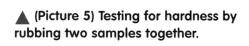

▲ (Picture 5) Testing for hardness by rubbing two samples together.

Summary
• Hard rocks are useful as building materials.
• Soft rocks are rarely used for building.
• Rock hardness can be tested by rubbing.

9

Weblink: www.curriculumvisions.com

Rocks shape the land

The shape of the land is often similar to the pattern of the hard and soft rocks below it.

Rocks lie beneath everything, so if you look around from, say, a hilltop, the shape of the land is often made by the shape of the rocks below.

Flat rocks

Rocks that lie in flat sheets make tablelands (Picture 1). If they are cut into by rivers or the sea, then the hard layers of rock make tall cliffs, while the soft layers of rock form more gentle slopes.

Sloping rocks

When sloping rocks lie underground, the pattern of hills and valleys tells us where the hard and softer bands of rock are found (Picture 2). The hills match the bands of hard rock, while the valleys match the bands of soft rock.

▼ **(Picture 1) This flat-topped land in a desert is called a tableland. Beneath it there are layers of flat rock. Notice how the cliff is made of just one kind of rock. This is a very hard rock.**

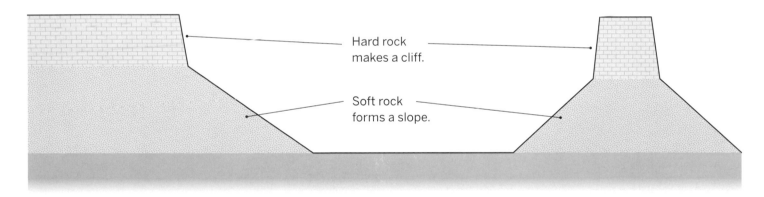

Hard rock makes a cliff.

Soft rock forms a slope.

Weblink: www.curriculumvisions.com

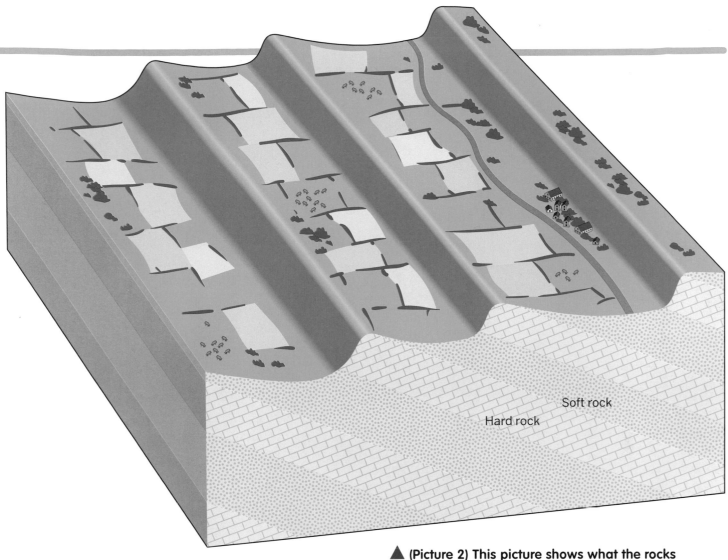

Soft rock

Hard rock

▲ (Picture 2) This picture shows what the rocks might be like under a land of hills and valleys.

Notice that the flatter parts are used for farming because this is where soils are thickest.

Old volcanoes

The original pipe that fed lava during a volcanic eruption fills up with lava as the volcano goes silent. This lava is hard and often remains as a pillar of rock (Picture 3).

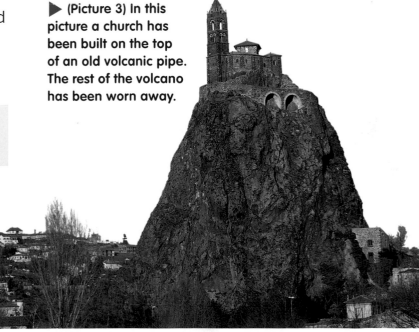

▶ (Picture 3) In this picture a church has been built on the top of an old volcanic pipe. The rest of the volcano has been worn away.

 How are rocks arranged when we see tablelands?

Summary
- Hard rocks form hills.
- Soft rocks form valleys.
- Flat sheets of rock make tablelands.

Weblink: www.curriculumvisions.com

Rocks that soak up water

LIMESTONE rocks soak up water quickly. Most other rocks are waterproof.

Over time, water destroys all rocks, turning them into soil. If water cannot get inside a rock, then the rock is destroyed very slowly. However, some rocks soak up or **ABSORB** water. When they do this they can be destroyed very quickly.

Why rocks soak up water

Water will flow into any small crack and hole in a rock. However, some rocks – volcanic rocks like granite and baked rocks like **SLATE** and marble – have no gaps and so are waterproof (Picture 1A). But other rocks have just the right-sized holes for water to flow into. Water soaks into these rocks just as it does in a sponge.

The rocks that soak up water most easily are **CHALK** and **SANDSTONE** (Picture 1B).

▼ **(Picture 1) A simple test will show which rocks are waterproof and which soak up water. Add small drops of water to the rock and see if the water soaks in.**

A

When water is slowly dripped onto a block of slate, the water runs off. This is why slate is used as a roofing stone.

B

When water is added a drop at a time to a block of chalk, it soaks in.

Weblink: www.curriculumvisions.com

Why rocks crumble

When rocks soak up water and then freeze, they crumble easily. You can see why this happens by putting a bag of wetted chalk in a freezer and letting it freeze (Picture 2). The water expands as it freezes, breaking the chalk apart.

Why rocks get eaten away

Rain contains chemicals (called **ACIDS**) that can slowly eat away some rocks. Acids work most quickly on soft rocks such as chalk and limestone. Some sandstones are also held together by a natural cement. When acid is added this cement is eaten away. Over time, limestone will completely disappear, while sandstone will fall apart. You can see this working by putting a block of chalk in some vinegar, which is also an acid (Picture 3).

◀ (Picture 2) Soak a small piece of chalk in water and then put it in a plastic bag in a freezer. Take the sample out of the bag and allow it to thaw. The freezing water cracks the rock apart. When the chalk is allowed to thaw the rock crumbles.

 What is the word for 'to soak up'?

Vinegar

Chalk

▲ (Picture 3) Take a small piece of chalk and put it in a glass with some vinegar. The vinegar is an acid so the chalk will slowly disappear.

Summary
- Chalks and sandstones can absorb water.
- Wet rocks that have soaked up water crumble if they freeze.
- Chalks and limestones can be eaten away by acids.

Weblink: www.curriculumvisions.com

How rocks are used

Hard rocks have many uses. They are used to make all types of buildings, and even to make roads.

▼ (Picture 1) Some of the many uses for stone can be seen in ancient as well as modern buildings.

Blocks of rock that are cut from a quarry are called **STONE**. People have found hard stone a very useful material for thousands of years (Picture 1). It is still used in huge amounts even today.

In the past, the only long-lasting building material was stone. All important buildings, such as cathedrals, palaces and temples, were made of stone. Stone was also used by wealthy people for their houses.

Building stone

Some stone, such as **LIMESTONE**, can be cut into in large blocks. This makes it especially useful for building (Pictures 2 and 3).

Roofing (slate)

Walls (marble)

Columns (limestone)

Steps (sandstone)

Road surface (lava)

Road foundations (limestone)

Weblink: www.curriculumvisions.com

Some stone, such as slate, breaks up into sheets. This can be used as thin slabs to make roofs.

Some stone, such as granite and marble, looks very attractive when it is polished. These types of stone are often used for decoration as statues, floors or the outside of buildings.

Road stone

Roads have to take the weight of lorries and be hard wearing. They are mainly made of hard stone.

For this purpose, the stone is quarried using explosives, then it is crushed up. Large pieces are used as foundations for roads. Small pieces are covered in tar and used to make the road surface.

▲ (Picture 2) This building uses limestone blocks for the walls.

▼ (Picture 3) Any hard stone can be used to make walls. This is limestone. This type of wall is called a dry stone wall because no cement has been used between the blocks.

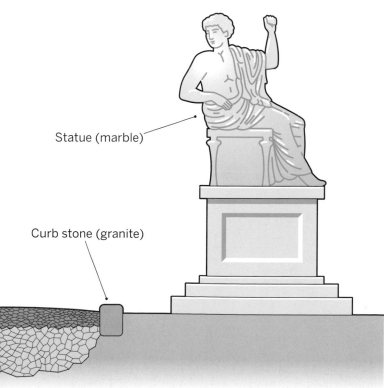

Statue (marble)

Curb stone (granite)

Q What rocks were used to make temples?

Summary
- Only hard rock is useful for building.
- Rocks that can be cut into shapes are used for building.
- Pieces of hard rock are used for roads.

Weblink: www.curriculumvisions.com

Artificial rocks

The main artificial rocks are bricks and concrete. They are easier to use for building than natural stone.

Building stone is expensive to quarry and difficult to cut into the right shapes. This is why, for thousands of years, people have made artificial rocks. We use them for building materials. The most common are **BRICKS** and **CONCRETE**.

Bricks

Bricks begin as **CLAY**. Clay is a soft, sticky material when wet, but as it dries it begins to get very hard. The simplest bricks are wet clay shaped into a brick and allowed to dry in the sun.

These kinds of bricks are only suited to very dry places because rain will make them wet and they will fall apart. But if the clay is baked, then it will become hard, strong and waterproof. This makes true bricks.

Bricks are used mainly for walls (Picture 1). They are also sometimes used for pavements (Picture 2).

Concrete

Concrete is a mixture of sand, cement and stones. The stones give the concrete its strength and the cement binds them together.

The advantage of concrete is that it can be poured into moulds and made to take on any shape (Pictures 2 and 3).

 What is a hard material baked from soft clay?

◀ (Picture 1) Bricks are cemented into place in an overlapping pattern to make the wall strong.

Weblink: www.curriculumvisions.com

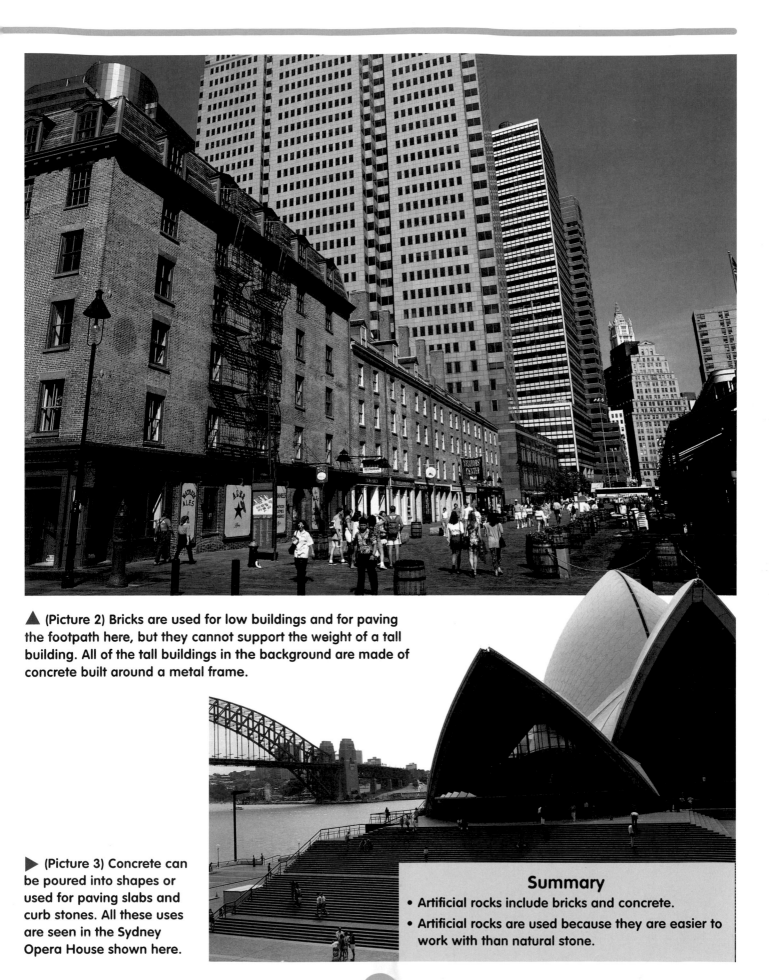

▲ (Picture 2) Bricks are used for low buildings and for paving the footpath here, but they cannot support the weight of a tall building. All of the tall buildings in the background are made of concrete built around a metal frame.

▶ (Picture 3) Concrete can be poured into shapes or used for paving slabs and curb stones. All these uses are seen in the Sydney Opera House shown here.

Summary
- Artificial rocks include bricks and concrete.
- Artificial rocks are used because they are easier to work with than natural stone.

17

Pebbles, sand and clay

As rocks roll down river beds, they get broken down into smaller pieces. We call these pieces pebbles, sand and clay.

The bed of most rivers is covered with small pieces of rock that have been worn into rounded shapes.

Pebbles, sand and clay

The large pieces of rounded rock we call **PEBBLES**. They are big enough for us to see that they are made of rock.

Sand is too small for you to see that it is made of rock (Picture 1). But when rubbed between the fingers it feels rough, or gritty.

The finest pieces of rock are called mud or clay. You cannot see these grains because they are too small. They are what make water look muddy.

How rock is made smaller

All pebbles, sand and clay start out as rock. The force of water in rivers and streams carries rocks along, bouncing them along the river bed (Picture 2A) so they crash into one another and the river bed. Each crash breaks off small chips from the corners or edges.

In time the rocks get smaller and more rounded (Picture 2B). The chippings may make sand, while the chipped rock becomes a pebble.

Bouncing, crashing and chipping continue, so that rocks become smaller as they get farther down the river. If you look in the banks of a river you can often see all three types of material together (Picture 3).

◀ (Picture 1) Here you can see pebbles (bottom left) and sand (top right).

 What does a pothole show us?

Weblink: www.curriculumvisions.com

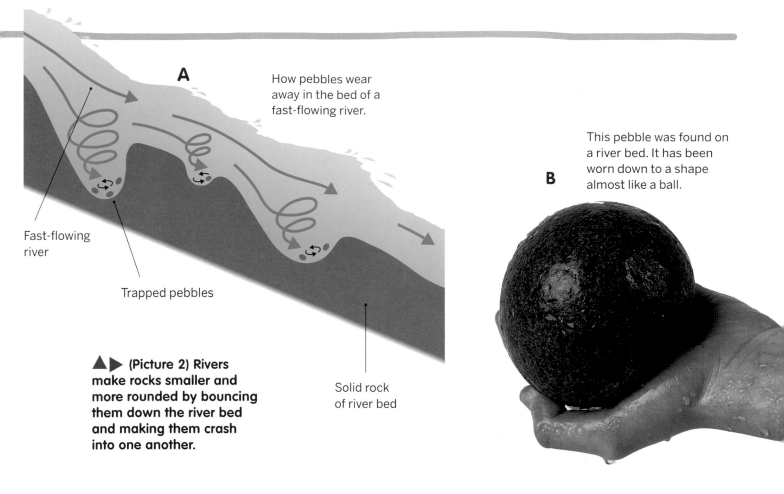

A

How pebbles wear away in the bed of a fast-flowing river.

Fast-flowing river

Trapped pebbles

Solid rock of river bed

B

This pebble was found on a river bed. It has been worn down to a shape almost like a ball.

▲▶ (Picture 2) Rivers make rocks smaller and more rounded by bouncing them down the river bed and making them crash into one another.

▲ (Picture 3) Pebbles, sand and clay occur in this river bank. If you were to take a sample and shake it in water, you would see the three types separate out.

Summary

- Pebbles, sand and clay are different sizes of rock worn down by rivers.
- As rock becomes worn down, so it becomes more rounded.

Weblink: www.curriculumvisions.com

Soils from rocks

Soils are made from rocks, but they are not hard like rocks.

Rocks are tough materials, but as they break down into smaller pieces, they make a thin layer on the surface. This is called a soil.

What is a soil made of?

A soil is a mixture of materials. It contains mostly fine pieces of rock such as clay and sand. It may also contain a few stones.

But if this was all there was, it would not be a soil. A soil also contains plant and animal remains. So a soil is a mixture of rock, and plant and animal remains.

Soil layers

Soils form in layers (Picture 1).

The top layer of the soil is called the **TOPSOIL**. It is dark in colour. Here you find clay, sand and plant roots.

▼▶ (Picture 1) Soils form in layers. The soil is quite thin and rests on solid rock.

Topsoil, dark in colour and where most plants put their roots.

Subsoil, lighter than the topsoil. Contains a few stones but no solid rock.

The rock from which the soil has formed.

Weblink: www.curriculumvisions.com

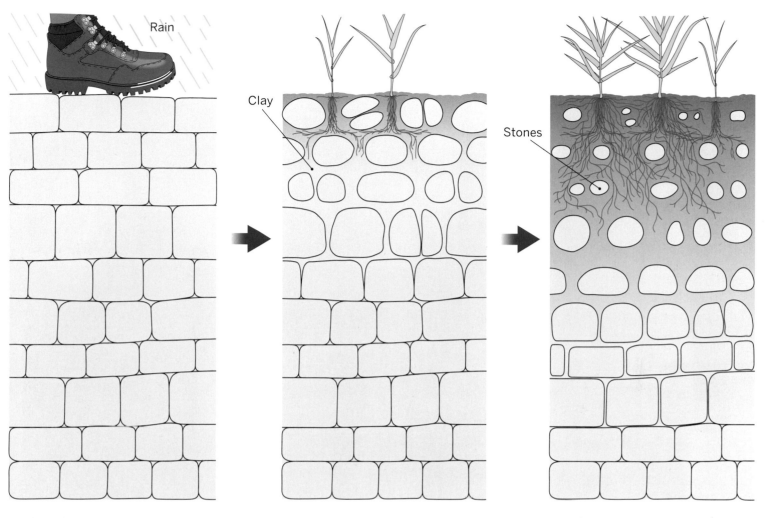

Rain

Clay

Stones

▲ (Picture 2) Rain falling onto rock soaks in and begins to destroy it. This leaves sand and clay behind. The stones are the remains of the original rock.

Below the topsoil is a lighter layer. This is the **SUBSOIL**. Few plant roots are found here. The subsoil rests on the solid rock.

How soils form

Soils form as rainwater causes the rock to break up (Picture 2).

You can think of the way soil is made from rock by comparing the way brown rust forms on a nail. As the nail is attacked by the weather, it becomes soft and flaky. When rock is attacked by the weather, it too becomes soft and loose.

Rocks, like nails, contain iron and so they also turn brown when breaking up into soils as a result of attacks by the weather.

Q **What is in topsoil?**

Summary
• Soils form in layers.
• Soils form above rocks.
• Soils are produced when rocks are attacked by the weather.

Weblink: www.curriculumvisions.com

Soils and water

Some soils let water pass quickly through them. They get dry and dusty easily in summer. Other soils hold the water for plants to use.

Have you ever seen countryside or school playing fields covered with water? These soils are waterlogged – they can't let the rainwater seep through fast enough.

Have you ever noticed that the grass dries out and goes brown in some parts of a playing field during the summer, while it stays green elsewhere? Soils which dry out quickly can't store enough water for plants during a drought.

To know why some soils become waterlogged and why others dry out quickly, you need to investigate the way water passes through a soil (Picture 1).

How water flows through soils

A soil is made of many tiny grains packed together (Picture 2).

If all the grains are small, they pack together very well, leaving only small gaps in-between. It is hard for water to squeeze through these tiny spaces. Instead, the water seeps in and gets stuck inside. Clay soils are made of tiny grains. Clay soils easily fill up with water and become waterlogged.

If all the grains are large, the gaps between them are large, so that water easily flows through. But very little water is trapped. Sandy soils are made of large grains and so they easily dry out.

If there is a mixture of soil grains, then there are some big gaps which let the water flow through, but some small ones to store water,

too. These are the best kinds of soils. A soil with a mixture of all kinds of sizes is known as **LOAM**.

Q Is clay the best or worst at letting water soak through?

A
Sand

▼ (Picture 1) This fair test was set up to see how water passed through different soils.

Three pots of the same size and with the same sized drainage holes were filled with the same amounts of different soils. The same amount of water was added to each soil and each soil was allowed to drain the water for the same amount of time. The amount of water that passed through the soil in this time showed how well the soil drained.

The results show that a sandy soil drains quickly (A), while a clay soil drains slowly (B). Neither is a good soil. What is needed is a loam soil that drains well but holds some water (C).

B
Clay

C
Loam
(sand and clay mix)

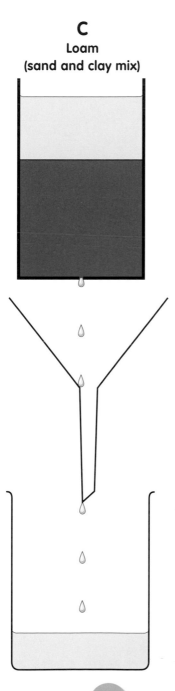

▲▼ (Picture 2) The gaps between sand grains are large. The gaps between clay grains are small.

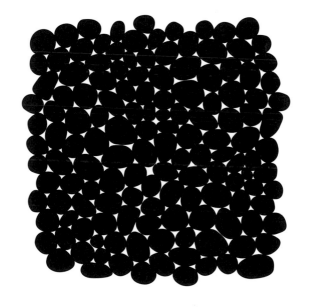

Summary
- Sandy soils do not hold water well.
- Clay soils fill up with water.
- Loam soils drain well and keep back enough water for plants.

Weblink: www.curriculumvisions.com

Index

Absorb 2, 12

Acid 2, 13

Artificial 16

Brick 2, 16–17

Cement 2, 8–9, 13, 15, 16

Chalk 2, 9, 12–13

Clay 2, 8, 16, 18–19, 20–21, 22–23

Concrete 2, 16–17

Granite 2, 7, 12, 15

Lava 2, 6–7, 11, 14

Limestone 2, 9, 12–13, 14–15

Loam 2, 22–23

Marble 2, 9, 12, 14–15

Mud 2, 8, 18, 20

Mudstone 8

Pebbles 2, 18–19

Quarry 2, 4–5, 15, 16

Rock 2, 4–5, 6–7, 8–9, 10–11, 12–13, 14, 16, 18–19, 20–21

Sand 2, 8–9, 16, 18–19, 20–21, 22–23

Sandstone 2, 8, 12–13, 14

Slate 2, 12, 14–15

Soil 2, 4–5, 11, 12, 20–21, 22–23

Stone 2, 12, 14–15, 16–17, 20–21

Subsoil 2, 20 21

Tableland 10–11

Topsoil 2, 20–21

Volcano 6–7, 8, 11

Waterproof 12, 16

Waterlogged 22–23

Curriculum Visions

Science@School

Pure inspiration

There is a Teacher's Guide which can be purchased to accompany this book. There is also comprehensive online support (including teacher's photocopiables and comprehension workbooks) supporting all aspects of the new Primary Curriculum. We publish, either printed or digitally, over 500 books to support Primary needs, in Geography, History, Religion, MFL, Maths, English and more at:

www.CurriculumVisions.com

(a subscription website)

This New Curriculum edition © Atlantic Europe Publishing 2014

The right of Brian Knapp to be identified as the author of this work has been asserted by him in accordance with the Copyright, Designs and Patents Act 1988.

Author
Brian Knapp, BSc, PhD

Educational Consultant
Peter Riley, BSc, C Biol, MI Biol, PGCE

Senior Designer
Adele Humphries, BA, PGCE

Editors
Lisa Magloff, MA, and Gillian Gatehouse

Illustrations
David Woodroffe

Designed and produced by
Atlantic Europe Publishing

Printed in China by
WKT Company Ltd

Rocks and soils – Curriculum Visions Science@School
A CIP record for this book is available from the British Library.

Paperback ISBN 978 1 78278 043 4

Picture credits
All photographs are from the Earthscape and Shutterstock picture libraries, except the following: (c=centre t=top b=bottom l=left r=right) *USGS* 1, 6b, 7tr.

This product is manufactured from sustainable managed forests. For every tree cut down at least one more is planted.